# Songs of Praise

Copyright © CWR 2015
Published 2015 by CWR, Waverley Abbey House, Waverley Lane, Farnham,
Surrey GU9 8EP, UK
Tel: 01252 784700 Email: mail@cwr.org.uk Registered Charity No. 294387
Registered Limited Company No. 1990308
Front cover image: Getty/Mark Bridger
Concept development, editing, design and production by CWR.
Printed in England by Linney Print.
All rights reserved. No part of this publication may be reproduced, stored in
a retrieval system, or transmitted, in any form or by any means, electronic,
mechanical, photocopying, recording or otherwise, without the prior
permission in writing of CWR.
Unless otherwise indicated, all Scripture references are from The Holy Bible,
New International Version (Anglicised edition), copyright © 1979, 1984,
2011 by Biblica (formerly International Bible Society).
Scripture is also taken from The Authorized (King James) Version. Rights in the
Authorized Version in the United Kingdom are vested in the Crown. Reproduced
by permission of the Crown's patentee, Cambridge University Press.

MIX
Paper from
responsible sources
FSC® C015900

# HOW TO GET THE BEST OUT OF
## *LIFE EVERY DAY*

### HERE ARE A FEW SUGGESTIONS:

- Ideally, carve out a regular time and place each day, with as few distractions as possible. Ask God what He has to say to you.

- Read the Bible passages suggested in the 'READ' references. (As tempting as it is, try not to skip the Bible reading and get straight into the notes.)

- The 'FOCUS' reference then gives you one or two verses to look at in more detail. Consider what the reading is saying to you and what challenges that may bring.

- Each day's comments are part of an overall theme. Try to recall what you read the previous day so that you maintain a sense of continuity.

- Spend time thinking about how to apply what God has said to you. Ask Him to help you do this.

- Pray the prayer at the end as if it were your own. Perhaps add your own prayer in response to what you have read and been thinking about.

Join in the conversation on Facebook
**www.facebook.com/jefflucasuk**

# A dawn chorus

From the first moment of creation, when God spoke the universe into being, there has been a song. Our minds can't begin to fathom the fabulous work that was done as He established light, colour, earth, air, water and the DNA of every living thing – but as all of this was formed, angels cheered and shouted for joy as the heavens joined in.

Later translations of Job say that the morning stars 'shone' together – stars don't actually hum along to a tune, though they do emit a frequency or hum that can be picked up by scientists – and elsewhere we read that the stars 'sing' God's praises – 'Praise him, sun and moon; praise him, all you shining stars' (Psa. 148:3).

This statement about a creation song in the book of Job is not just a snapshot of the epic joy that accompanied the beginning of everything, but is a reminder to Job – and to us – that we are all mere mortals, incapable of being able to grasp so many mysteries about God and about life and about the universe.

As Job hears about that first awesome song, he has to face the question, even in his acute suffering – where were you when all this happened?

The beauty of creation should prompt songs of praise from us. Our songs should be expressions of truth, praise and thankfulness as we realise our own incapacity to grasp the magnitude of God. Sing a song of thanksgiving – and trust – today.

**Prayer: Mighty, awesome God, thank You for Your creation, which declares Your praises. Help me to join in with the song today. Amen.**

**READ:**
**Job 38:1–7**
**Psalm 19:1–4**

**FOCUS**
*'while the morning stars sang together and all the angels shouted for joy'*
*(Job 38:7)*

The beauty of creation should prompt songs of praise

**READ:**
Psalm 42:1–6 //
Jeremiah 18:13–15

Weekend

# Focused remembering

Regular readers of *Life Every Day* will recall that last month I mentioned the importance and power of remembering. But it's appropriate that we return to it briefly today, especially as we still stand on the threshold of a new year. The psalmist strengthened his soul for the present day by looking back at past days. This was not sentimental nostalgia, a hankering for what will never be again, but focused recall. He remembers the joy of being together with God's people, the divine protection that he experienced and the exciting days when he'd shout the praises of God out loud.

There are so many episodes of my life that I simply cannot remember now. They are filed away, archived in my mind and recalled by shared conversation, but often forgotten. And that means I've let slip some of the joys of the past that might prompt gratitude, or mislaid lessons learned, so that I foolishly have to learn them all over again. That's why I'm suggesting that we might want to consider journalling as we navigate through another 12 months; that we might remember and be stronger in faith as we do.

**To ponder: Why not ask the Lord if there is something specific that He would like you to remember as you move forward into this new year?**

we might remember and be
stronger in faith as we do

# Transformed in God's presence

A t midnight on New Year's Eve, millions toasted the passing of what was a very challenging year and celebrated the possibilities of an unsullied 2016. Resolutions were made as some determined to exercise more, eat less and embrace or discard a host of helpful or destructive habits. In short, we hope for change in our world, in our communities and in our personal lives. But do people really change, or do we generally amble through life with a few radical revisions after coming to Christ, but settling into a cruise control mentality thereafter?

The psalmist is telling us that change is possible – in fact, we can navigate through changing attitudes even as we pray, reflect and praise. That's what happens here. Apparently longing to be part of Temple worship again in Jerusalem, the writer begins by pouring out his heart, saying how he thirsts for God's presence. Then he deliberately remembers better days in his past, days of worship and celebration with God's people. But then he stirs himself and challenges his own heart, demanding to know why he was allowing himself to be so downcast and determining to put his hope in God. Prayerful reflection is not just a static religious habit, or a 'quiet time' for the sake of ticking a religious box, but can be a way of journeying and changing as we look back, look within and look forward with determined choices. This year, let's be people who grow and change because of times of dynamic reflection. That will make success with those new year resolutions a lot more likely.

**Prayer: As the deer pants for streams of water, so my soul pants for You, my God. This year, Lord, continue to transform me by Your Spirit as I seek Your face. Amen.**

**READ:**
**Psalm 42:1–11**
**2 Corinthians 3:17–18**

**FOCUS**
*'These things I remember as I pour out my soul: how I used to go to the house of God under the protection of the Mighty One'*
*(Psa. 42:4)*

# Thirsty for God

**READ:**
**Psalm 143:1–6**
**Philippians 3:1–14**

**FOCUS**
*'I thirst for you like a parched land.'*
(Psa. 143:6)

Setting out on a five-mile walk, we became somewhat over-enthusiastic as we enjoyed the scenery and so, in burning noon-day heat, we turned it into a 13-mile hike. Unfortunately we didn't take water with us, so we soon began to feel dehydrated. Our minuscule experience of thirst taught us that it's not a good feeling. There are many in the world who really know what it is to thirst.

We saw over the last couple of days that the writer of Psalm 42 was thirsty for God and now, as we turn to a psalm of David, we hear a similar cry. He is thirsty for God, like a parched man stranded in a searing desert.

I find it hard to fully identify with David's words. I don't thirst for God with the intensity that is expressed in this psalm. Sometimes I can crave the blessing of God, the answer to that deadlock situation, healing for someone I love who is struggling with a life-threatening illness, or even direction and guidance when I'm not sure what to do. But David is crying out for God Himself, for God's presence, for the face of God and not just the hand of God.

Frankly, I confess that I don't feel that thirst and can so easily exist with basic prayer habits, without spending time and effort in wanting to draw close to God and know Him more. Paul, like David, obviously had that thirst and viewed knowing God more as his number one priority. And so today, for me and for you, in this new year, I'm praying a strange prayer: I thirst to be thirsty for God.

I thirst to be thirsty

**Prayer: Lord, I want to say 'I thirst for You like a parched land'. Create a new hunger and thirst in me for You, for Your presence, that I might know You more. Amen.**

# CWR MINISTRY EVENTS

Please pray for the team

| DATE | EVENT | PLACE | PRESENTER(S) |
|------|-------|-------|--------------|
| 21 Jan | Quiet Day for Pastoral Carers | Waverley Abbey House | Andy Peck |
| 25-29 Jan | January Bargain Break | Pilgrim Hall | Pilgrim Hall Staff |
| 28 Jan | Refreshing Your Spiritual Life | WAH | Andy Peck |
| 4 Feb | The Bible in a Day | WAH | Andy Peck |
| 11 Feb | Discipleship Forum | Woodlands Church, Bristol | Tony Pullin, Andy Peck, Dave Mitchell and Lucy Peppiatt |
| 12 Feb | Managing Our Time | WAH | Andy Peck |
| 16 Feb | Prayer Breakfast | PH | Pilgrim Hall Staff |
| 24 Feb | Church Leaders Forum | WAH | Andy Peck |
| 25 Feb | The Life and Times of Jesus | WAH | Andy Peck |
| 28 Feb | Alumni Event | WAH | Waverley Abbey College |

Please pray for our students and tutors on our ongoing BA Counselling programme at Waverley and Pilgrim Hall, as well as our Certificate and Diploma of Christian Counselling and MA in Christian Counselling qualifications.

We would also appreciate prayer for our ministry in Singapore as well as our many regional events that we are embarking on this year.

For further information and a full list of CWR's courses, phone **+44 (0)1252 784719** or visit the CWR website **www.cwr.org.uk**

You can also download our free daily Prayer Track from **www.cwr.org.uk/free-resources**

www.cwr.org.uk

# Help me

READ:
**Psalm 143:1–12**
**Matthew 6:5–15**

**FOCUS**
*'Let the morning bring me word of your unfailing love, for I have put my trust in you. Show me the way I should go, for to you I entrust my life.'*
(Psa. 143:8)

Jesus had to deal with mistaken notions about prayer. I love the fact that Jesus exposed the Pharisees with their love of showy, lengthy prayers; although Jesus taught persistence in prayer, which calls us to repetitively bring our requests to God, He also taught against 'babbling' prayer, which focuses more on the number of words spoken or the length of time taken, rather than authentic, heartfelt prayer. As David calls out to God, he pictures a penitent Temple attender waiting to hear from the priests the next morning. His words are a breathless series of urgent, desperate pleas, all of which can be summarised in one word – help!

Help. Sometimes that's the only word we can pray and the only word we need to pray. I've prayed it often, sometimes in a high-pitched voice.

But notice too how 'me'-focused this call for help is – the psalmist is completely engrossed in his own fears, needs and concerns. It's helpful to notice this, because even though some of us can tend towards being too self-centred in our praying, there are others who, in the opposite extreme, feel nervous about praying for themselves. I discovered this when I asked a Christian businessman if he prayed regularly about his business dealings, which is obviously a good thing to do. He told me that he'd always felt that it was inappropriate to do so, as if to pray for his own life and needs was inappropriate. Don't be afraid to yell help. And don't be reluctant to yell 'Help me'.

**Prayer: Lord, teach me to do Your will, for You are my God; may Your good Spirit lead me on level ground. Please help me. Amen.**

Help. Sometimes that's the only word we can pray

# God is good

Regular readers will know that I often have to admit my failures, but here let me bare my heart about what is a personal preference. I'm not a great fan of those moments in services when the excited worship leader yells at the congregation, 'God is good!' and the congregation chirp back, 'All the time', whereupon the rather delighted aforementioned worship leader retorts with, 'All the time!', and the response comes back, 'God is good!'. It all seems a little cheesy to me. But despite my personal preference about this, the statement is theologically correct and in fact it's a great summary about the character of God.

While dedicating the Temple in a time of great excitement and joy, and then being visited by the very presence of God, Solomon's musicians had only one sentence they could sing about the Lord: 'He is good; his love endures for ever' (2 Chron. 5:13). Good can sound a little vague. Goodness here means mercy, generosity and covenant loyalty. Sometimes we don't understand God and wish that life was not as it is. There are seasons when we wonder why the good God doesn't intervene more. But in one of the shortest songs in the Bible, Solomon's band strikes up the tune that we'd do well to join in with: God is good when life is bad. And that isn't going to change. Throughout eternity, His goodness will endure – forever. Human relationships can be fickle and fragile because people who used to be good, change. Love turns sour. But God is good and He will be. All the time.

**Prayer: Father, I thank You for Your steadfast love, Your consistent character, Your generous grace. Amen.**

**READ:**
**2 Chronicles 5:1–14**
**Psalm 136:1**

**FOCUS**
*'He is good; his love endures for ever.'*
*(2 Chron. 5:13)*

# A lawsuit song

**READ:**
Deuteronomy
31:14–32:2
Hosea 6:3

**FOCUS**
*'Let my teaching
fall like rain and my
words descend like
dew, like showers
on new grass, like
abundant rain on
tender plants.'*
(Deut. 32:2)

I've been pondering: if I knew my next sermon would be my last, what would I say? This is Moses' last address to Israel and it's not an entirely upbeat message. On the contrary, scholars see this as a 'lawsuit song' as God brings charges against His wayward people. The song begins beautifully, speaking of the Word of the Lord being like refreshing rain or dew, providing vital nourishment to the plants and the land. The imagery would have brought a smile to the hearts and faces of the Israelites, who lived in a land where rain was scarce and valuable. Even though Moses would go on to sing some difficult, challenging words, he prefaces his song by speaking about refreshment and nourishment.

And that's my experience of the Bible. Living for Christ can be tiring, tedious and seemingly unrewarding at times. But when I bring my heart and mind to Scripture, allowing its truth to wash over me, refresh my memories, warm my heart, instil me with courage and renew my vision, it is like rain in the desert. Hosea speaks of the coming of God in the same way.

Ironically, it's in the seasons when I'm most thirsty – we talked about that earlier – that I feel less inclined to drink. When life is bruising, when I'm disappointed in others and especially disappointed with myself, it's then that I am less likely to turn to Scripture. But discipline brings me back to that life-giving Word, even if the Word brings rebuke, as Moses' song does. When thirsty, let's drink.

**Prayer: Your Word brings life, Lord. Help me to find nourishment and refreshment in it today. Amen.**

# God, the rock

READ:
Deuteronomy
32:1–4 //
Psalm 95:1–11

Yesterday, a childhood friend posted photographs online of the park where we used to play over four decades ago. Everything changes. And it's not only the geography that has changed. As young children, we used to go to that park, unaccompanied and play all day, generally without any fear for our safety. How culture has changed.

And recently I learned of a ministry colleague who has made some tragic moral choices. He seemed so dependable. His sad choices came as a shock.

In Moses' song, he celebrates the truth that God is like a rock. Using a familiar analogy that the Israelites could immediately relate to – they lived in rocky terrain – Moses was not suggesting that God is static, but rather that He is consistent, always faithful, certain to keep His promises – as we saw, His love endures. And as Moses celebrates God's consistency, he contrasts that with Israel's fickleness.

There is One who is unfailingly consistent. Thank God.

**To ponder: Can you think of times when the truth that God is dependable and consistent was of help to you? What does that truth mean to you today?**

There is One who is
unfailingly consistent

**FOCUS**
*'Is this the way you
repay the LORD, you
foolish and unwise
people?' (Deut. 32:6)*

# A strange, sad song

If I do something sacrificial for someone, I don't need to be celebrated, but appreciation matters. A lack of appreciation seems to cheapen the gift.

The songs that we sing are usually happy and they tend to rightly focus on God and who He is rather than on us. But in this strange song, the faults of Israel are listed with words that don't spare their blushes and one of the most telling indictments is this: they are an ungrateful people and have 'repaid' God with rebellion and ongoing sin. They are like rebellious children who ignore and reject the tender care of their parents.

We can never pay God back for our salvation – it's free and the price has been paid in full, in a way that we cannot fully understand, by Jesus at the cross. But we cannot only express our gratitude in the worship we bring, but in the lives that we live. Moses' song affirms this truth – God is our maker. We belong to Him. To accept grace and then deliberately turn around and commit to life choices that we know displease Him is terrible 'repayment' indeed.

Jesus clearly taught that thankfulness and gratitude were to be celebrated. And He was amazed when people who had experienced incredible healing, like some who had suffered from leprosy, were so amiss in their not bothering to come back and express thanks. They repaid Him with apparent indifference. I'm challenged to root out those attitudes and habits in my life that run roughshod over God's grace. How about you?

thankfulness and gratitude were to be celebrated

**Prayer: Save me, Lord, from ever 'repaying' You with stubbornness or ingratitude. Thank You for Your faithful love. Amen.**

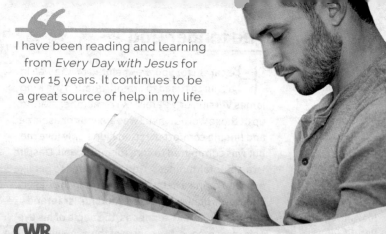

I have been reading and learning from *Every Day with Jesus* for over 15 years. It continues to be a great source of help in my life.

**CWR**
Transforming lives through ...

# Published Resources

For over 50 years, CWR has sought to provide resources that help people of all ages and backgrounds to understand the Bible and apply it to their own lives and relationships. We provide a variety of seven dated Bible reading notes to 'feed the whole family', reaching readers around the world, every day.

Our books, DVDs and church programmes also help hundreds of churches and individuals to access life-changing teaching and encouragement, through both print and digital materials. Let your life become transformed and join in – individually or with your church.

**www.cwr.org.uk/booksanddvds**

# The tender God

**FOCUS**
*'In a desert land
he found him, in a
barren and howling
waste. He shielded
him and cared for
him; he guarded him
as the apple of his
eye' (Deut. 32:10)*

'He careth for you' was painted on the wall in a church I used to attend, quoting the King James Version of 1 Peter 5:7. I remember staring up at those words when I was anxious or ashamed and finding comfort that God didn't only love me, but was committed to care for me as well. Despite Israel's unfaithfulness, God had tended to her like one who found a helpless wanderer in the desert. The words picture God 'surrounding' Israel and 'attentively caring' for her as 'the apple of his eye'. This term means 'the centre of the eye', which is the most valuable part – without it, there is no sight.

Then the imagery shifts, this time to picture an eagle helping to train a young eaglet to fly. Even as she nudges the bird out of the nest, she hovers protectively. This tender language is echoed by the prophet Hosea, seeing God as the Father who tenderly looks after Israel like a small child (Hosea 11).

Sometimes people paint God as dispassionate, unable to be moved because to be impacted by what people do would weaken Him. But that's not the biblical picture of God. God's heart soars – and breaks – over His people.

All that God did for Israel should have compelled them to avoid and shun foreign gods. But they failed and were unfaithful in spite of His faithfulness. Are there foreign gods in our lives? Let's abandon them and turn again to the God who tenderly cares for us and cares about us.

**Prayer: You care for me, Jesus. Thank You. Amen.**

God's heart
soars – and
breaks – over
His people

# A song of warning to the successful

READ:
**Deuteronomy 32:15**
**John 15:1–5**

**FOCUS**
*'Jeshurun grew fat and kicked; filled with food, they became heavy and sleek.' (Deut. 32:15)*

Enjoying a country rock concert recently (I never thought I'd write that sentence!), we were delighted with one of the support bands. Their music was catchy, memorable and they had a really pleasant stage presence. We were encouraged as we discovered that the band we enjoyed were Christians – I believe that the lead singer used to be involved in youth ministry. Later we were glad to hear that they had been nominated for a major music award – and then dismayed that they posted photos on their website of them getting drunk in celebration. I wondered how many young Christians were disappointed because success had spoiled those talented musicians, or so it seemed. I'm not here to judge. Who knows how any one of us might behave if we suddenly found ourselves with too much money or fame? But from this sad illustration and from this one verse from Moses' song, we learn that success can be perilous.

Moses sings about 'Jeshurun' (a poetic name for Israel) getting 'fat' and then turning to false gods. We see that when we are in need we're more likely to groan out for God's help and when we're in plenty we can more easily gloat, become self-sufficient and wander away. The picture of a grossly overfed beast, fattened up on plenty, is not a pretty one. I can look back on a few times when we, as a family, took major steps of faith where without God we would have been in trouble – but then, when our resources increased, my dependency decreased.

**Prayer: Help me to depend on You when all is well, as well as when it is not, Lord. Amen.**

# A jealous God

**FOCUS**
*'They made me jealous by what is no god and angered me with their worthless idols.' (Deut. 32:21)*

It will ultimately erode and even destroy any friendship or marriage. Jealousy is not usually seen as an attractive character trait. The jealous person is seen as possessive, controlling, usually has a wild imagination and is somewhat neurotic about the person that they say they love, but are obsessively jealous about. And then jealousy is often associated with envy, which is equally unattractive. So as Moses sings a song about a God who is jealous, what is he talking about? In the New Testament Paul talks about God's jealousy too, calling the Corinthians away from idolatry. God refuses to be just one of a selection of gods – He demands our undivided loyalty.

It's important that we realise that Israel's wandering from their allegiance to God was not only about them embracing an alternative spirituality. Bad ideas have terrible consequences and so it was with Israel. They had embraced nothing less than child sacrifice, the ritual offering of their children to their false gods. There is no way to describe the awfulness of this practice, as live children were tossed into the fires. No wonder the words that Moses uses mean 'worshipping demons'. Not only was it so barbaric, but it was all a total waste, because the words that Moses uses to describe the idols literally mean 'no gods'.

Jealousy is a sign of intense passion. God is not indifferent when we allow false idols into our lives. He covets our faithfulness to Him, because He knows what chaos allegiance to false gods will bring.

God is not indifferent

**Prayer: Today, may I be found loyal and faithful to You, loving God. Amen.**

# Songs of life

**READ:**
**Deuteronomy
30:15–18**
**Deuteronomy
32:42–47**

**FOCUS**
*'They are not just
idle words for you
– they are your life.'*
*(Deut. 32:47)*

In some church circles there's a tendency to minimise the importance of sung worship. The impression given is that sung worship is the warm-up, slightly more important than the announcements, but the real core business of the day is the preaching of Scripture. And I think that's a mistake. Our songs enable us to declare our faith with music that can move and stir our hearts too. There have been many times when I have dragged myself reluctantly into a church service, not feeling terribly interested or vibrant in faith (which is especially awkward when you feel like that and you happen to be the preacher!), but then well-phrased and skilfully arranged and performed words have lifted my soul once more. Life has come again.

As Moses tells the people that the words of his song are life, he's using the idea in a much deeper context – he wants them to know that the truths in his song are not abstract principles or empty theological notions but they are to direct them in their future.

We believers live with theories and there's always a danger that they descend into being just that – theories. But God's Word sung aloud has authority and would provide the source of life for Israel as they went into their land.

Perhaps we should ask God a question today: in my life, are there truths that have become 'idle words' because I might vaguely believe, but don't really endeavour to live in the good of them?

**Prayer: Help me to find my heart stirred in worship and
my heart changed as the truth that I sing is applied,
Lord. Amen.**

**READ:**
Exodus 15:1–18 //
Psalm 66:1–20

# An anthem

It's the first song recorded in detail in Scripture, although, as we saw, there was angelic singing at the moment of creation (Job 38:7). From the very beginning, singing has always been an appropriate response to God's goodness and power.

The 'Song of Moses' was a spontaneous song of praise that was sung by a chorus of millions, as the entire Hebrew nation joined in. Men like Moses sang alongside women like Miriam. God's song is inclusive. There's even a rabbinic tradition that the unborn embryos in the wombs of pregnant mothers sang along as well! God delivered His people from certain defeat, they saw what He had done and now bring Him this anthem of praise.

Many of the Bible's songs focus on what God has done and who He is, rather than who we are and what we feel about God. Sometimes I struggle to worship because I have to sing words that declare that I'm happy/excited/ready to dance when I am not in that emotional space at all. But the truth about God is unchanging and doesn't shift with our mood or circumstances. Perhaps we should sing more about God and less about what we *feel* about God.

**To ponder: 'Perhaps we should sing more about God and less about what we *feel* about God.' What do you think?**

God's song is inclusive

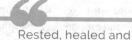

Rested, healed and
refreshed – in 48 hours.
Amazing value for money!

**CWR**

Transforming lives through ...

# Courses and Events

Investing in people's life, ministry and faith
through effective and valuable teaching
has always been at the heart of CWR. Our
courses and events provide a breadth and
depth of teaching to help you to learn,
whatever your church background, age
or experience. Bible Discovery, Life and
Discipleship, Inspiring Women, Pastoral
Leadership, Small Group Leadership
training and Insight Days are just some
of the areas in which we can help you
deepen your faith, instruct your mind,
inspire your heart and ignite your spirit.
Join us this year for an evening, one day,
weekend or week-long course.

**www.cwr.org.uk/training**

# Rescued

**FOCUS**
*'Pharaoh's chariots and his army he has hurled into the sea. The best of Pharaoh's officers are drowned in the Red Sea.'*
*(Exod. 15:4)*

The first song in Scripture focuses on this dominant theme: rescue. The song emphasises the mighty strength of the enemy that the Hebrews faced as they cowered before the might of Pharaoh's army. Highlighting the power of the Egyptians, Moses speaks of the chariots and 'the best of Pharaoh's officers'. This was not a rabble army of rookies that were defeated by God's intervention, it was a terrifying battalion of elite troops. But all were swept away. The Hebrews, unable to do anything to rescue themselves, were delivered. It was God's hand, God's breath, God's initiative that had brought about the triumph. At this stage in their history, the Hebrews didn't have to fight. Rather they just had to let God do the fighting and then they were called to celebrate and be grateful.

Too often my thanksgiving to God focuses on small mercies. I'm grateful for the safe drive home last night, for the sunshine, for the smiles of my grandsons and the devoted friendship of Kay, my wife. And I should be thankful for all of those blessings. But sometimes I forget this vital truth: I have been saved, rescued from the power of sin, snatched from the jaws of hopeless living and plucked from the certainty of judgment. Like the Hebrews, there was nothing I could do to rescue myself. All of my attempts at self-improvement, to justify myself before God – none of it would be of any use. We're not saved by our works, which cancels out any reason for boasting. But in Christ, I now have a salvation song to sing.

**Prayer: Lord God, You saved and rescued me, and I'm eternally grateful. Amen.**

# God has acted and God will act again

**READ:**
**Exodus 15:1–18**
**Hebrews 13:8**

**FOCUS**
*'In your unfailing love you will lead the people you have redeemed. In your strength you will guide them to your holy dwelling.'*
*(Exod. 15:13)*

In celebrating not just what God has done, but who He is, Moses' song then turns to the future and prophesies about how God will help the people as they continue their journey. They didn't see the Red Sea parting and the routing of the Egyptians as a one-off event but rather saw the future loaded with possibility because the Lord would continue to be with them. The fulfilment of those prophetic hopes is documented in the book of Joshua.

Recently I've been challenged by the thought that many of the great things that God has done in my life have been in the distant past. Perhaps a little cynicism has crept in, robbing me of the expectation of God's power and help that I should have for the future. When that happens, I find myself fretting about the future without too much prayer. The one human who boasted in his own self-sufficiency in this song was Pharaoh and things didn't go well for him as a result!

The God who has been with us will be with us tomorrow. Perhaps you're staring at a huge looming challenge and you're tempted to feel overwhelmed. God forbid that I should offer you a cliché today, but permit me to offer you a truth: God is mighty to save, He has been with you and He will be with you. Moses' song begins with a personal affirmation: the Lord is my strength and song. May you be able to make a similar, distinctly personal declaration about the God who is yours today.

**Prayer: Lord, You are my strength and song and whatever may come, You will be. Amen.**

God ... has been with you and He will be with you

# A repetitive song

**READ:**
Psalm 136:1–26
Romans 8:31–37

**FOCUS**
*'Give thanks to
the God of heaven.
His love endures
for ever.'*
(Psa. 136:26)

Incredibly, one commentator describes the English translation of this psalml as 'laboured' and even 'tedious'. I couldn't disagree more. The word that is translated 'love' is actually *hesed*, one of the most beautiful words in the Old Testament, more accurately translated as 'loving kindness'. The word not only speaks of kindness, one of God's attributes that is often overlooked, particularly by those who tend to view him primarily as a judge, but it also has strong roots in covenant relationships like marriage, which is a union begun and bound by solemn vows. God's love for us does not hinge on fickle emotions or changing moods, but is trustworthy because God has pledged that love forever and will not change His mind.

Paul also celebrates the tenacity and faithfulness of that love, celebrating the truth that nothing can ever separate us from it.

As we consider this liturgical psalm, with statements and responses clearly set out, it's as if God is repeating Himself over and over again, endeavouring to drum into our hearts and minds the truth that is sometimes difficult to grasp: we are loved by Him. There are times when I find it easier to believe that God loves the world generally rather than me, Jeff, specifically. Are you like me? When we fail, when our prayers seem ignored and heaven is apparently silent, when tragedy strikes without any sense of purpose of explanation, then we can become uncertain about God's love. Today, read that psalml through a few times and let the truth settle your heart: you are loved.

**Prayer: I give thanks to You, Lord of lords; Your love endures forever. You alone do great wonders, Your love endures forever. Amen.**

# Nothing shall separate us

Yesterday we saw that Paul echoed the psalmist's liturgical refrain about the enduring, steadfast, loving kindness of God. In what is not technically a song, but is worth looking at nevertheless, Paul celebrates the truth that nothing can separate us from that love and then begins to list some ten potential circumstances that might challenge that truth. We wonder if we're loved when death strikes, but Paul also includes life in his list. How wise he was to do that, because although fear of death can be real, fear of what life can bring can rob us of a sense of God's love too. Supernatural forces, angelic or demonic, can't pluck us out of His love either – perhaps Paul reiterates that truth a few words later when he mentions powers. Nor can the life we're experiencing now, nor the uncharted future, with all of its currently hidden challenges, separate us from that love. 'Height nor depth' is a strange phrase – some suggest that it means the vastness of the cosmos. When we look up at the stars, we feel very insignificant. Is it really true that there is a God who, in the midst of managing the immensity of the universe, knows us? Paul says that he is convinced that this is the case. And in using the term 'nor anything else in all creation', Paul abandons specifics and in one single sentence affirms this: nothing can separate us. His words are not cold theology, but designed to comfort and assure us. God's love is ours and nothing can snatch us away from it.

**Prayer: Lord, I am convinced that nothing in all creation will be able to separate me from the love of God that is in Christ Jesus. I give You thanks and praise. Amen.**

**READ:**
**Romans 5:8**
**Romans 8:38–39**

.......................................

**FOCUS**
*'neither height nor depth, nor anything else in all creation, will be able to separate us from the love of God that is in Christ Jesus our Lord.' (Rom. 8:39)*

God's love is ours

# A song in the midst of conflict

**READ:**
1 Samuel 1:1–20
2 Corinthians
11:16–29

**FOCUS**
*'Because the Lord had closed Hannah's womb, her rival kept provoking her in order to irritate her. This went on year after year.'*
(1 Sam. 1:6–7)

Some of the best songs come out of hardship and daily struggle. The spirituals that emerged from the terribly oppressed slaves in America demonstrate that anguish and despair often create deep, moving songs that powerfully express pain mingled with hope. Tomorrow we are going to look at the song of a woman who had known years of struggle – Hannah – but before we do it's good to reflect on her circumstances.

Hannah had multiple challenges. Barren in a culture that viewed an inability to bear children as the judgment of God, she lived in a household where she was irritated and provoked daily by an aggressive rival. Then it would appear that she had a rather insensitive husband too – his generosity to her provoked more conflict, so he was kind but clumsy and then he seemed to think that being married to him ably compensated for childlessness. He was not a man overly gifted with thoughtfulness and was perhaps deluded by an inflated opinion of himself. Couple that with being mistaken for a drunk when you pray and we can see that Hannah had to deal with more than her fair share of grinding pain.

All of this reminds us that we do faith in a real world, with all its disappointments, irritations and ongoing frustrations that seem unchangeable. But refusing to back away even when her prayers were misunderstood by watching humans, Hannah determined to trust in God regardless. If you find yourself in conflict and the struggle is daily and relentless, may God help you to sing nevertheless.

we do faith in a real world

**Prayer: In the midst of the joys and struggles of everyday life, help me to praise You, Lord. Amen.**

> The teaching has been amazing, very clear, challenging and full of content – inspiring!

**CWR**

Transforming lives through ...

# Waverley Abbey College

Over the last 30 years, CWR has pioneered and developed renowned expertise in the area of Christian counselling training, based on the Waverley Integrative Framework. Waverley Abbey College was established to provide Higher Education underpinned by a Christian worldview. The unique, rural settings of Waverley Abbey House and Pilgrim Hall create a personal atmosphere that enables intensive and challenging study to an outstanding academic level. Find out if this is for you by embarking on a 5-day starter course or applying directly for one of the Higher Education programmes – from a BA in Counselling to an MA Relational Counselling and Psychotherapy.

**www.waverleyabbeycollege.ac.uk**

# God is God

A few days ago we reflected on the truth that God is good. But as we begin to consider Hannah's song of praise, we hear the truth that sat at the very centre of Israel's understanding of their God, which is that He is the ultimate authority. God, quite simply, is God.

There's a danger that we can drift into trying to revise God, to make Him what we want Him to be and even to unconsciously airbrush out elements of His character that are not to our taste. If we don't like the idea of God calling anyone to account for their behaviour, then we can emphasise His love and acceptance and quietly ignore the truth that He is the holy One who not only loves, but sets boundaries and makes demands upon us. Or we can insist that culture has moved on and so think that what God has commanded in the past is no longer relevant. When we do this we practise what C.S. Lewis called 'Chroniclesological snobbery' – the notion that we know far better than our predecessors did, because we are more enlightened. This attempt to revise God is no new temptation – the Israelites tried it in their construction of the golden calf back in the days of the Exodus. The calf made no demands, was an object to bless them but had no capacity to judge them – and it was a totally false god, dead and worthless. Let's let God be God in our lives. He is who He is and will be what He will be.

**To ponder: Are there aspects of the character of God that you'd like to change? What are they and why?**

let God be God in our lives

Weekend

# The God of the turnaround

I recently heard news of a friend who is battling cancer. Over many years of ministry, Kay and I have got to know countless people around the world. Blessed with such a large number of friends, it's inevitable that we are going to hear both good and bad news. When the word 'cancer' is used, it generally strikes with such fear, even though modern medicine is often able to beat it completely. But there are times when the prognosis is very bad. That's when we can quickly surrender to believing that the disease is unbeatable and the outcome unavoidable.

While I am nervous of people who rush into declaring healing or assurance of future healing when they are actually just verbalising their hopes, let's remember that God is the God of the turnaround.

Hannah's situation was bleak, as we've seen. But as we consider the words of her song, we hear her celebrating the God who turns the tables, reversing the fortunes of those who had nothing and giving them everything and vice versa.

In her song, she talks about a king, even though there was no king in Israel at this time. Some scholars believe that she was prophetically speaking of the King to come, Jesus, even though she would not have been aware of it. The Early Church viewed that part of Hannah's song as a prophecy about Christ. There was more in her words than even she knew. If there's a situation in your life that calls for a radical turnaround, may you have faith to believe that God can do it.

**Prayer: Today, my heart rejoices in You, Lord, mighty God, for whom nothing is too hard. Help me to pray with faith and live in faithfulness. Amen.**

**READ:**
**1 Samuel 2:4–11**
**Jeremiah 32:26–27**

**FOCUS**
*'The bows of the warriors are broken, but those who stumbled are armed with strength. Those who were full hire themselves out for food, but those who were hungry are hungry no more.'*
*(1 Sam. 2:4–5)*

# Boasting in God

**READ:**
1 Samuel 2:1–11
James 4:13–17

**FOCUS**
*'Then Hannah prayed and said: "My heart rejoices in the Lord; in the Lord my horn is lifted high. My mouth boasts over my enemies, for I delight in your deliverance."'*
*(1 Sam. 2:1–2)*

Name-dropping is a really jarring habit. Perhaps you know someone who does it. They delight in mentioning how many famous people they have been hobnobbing with. And although the habit is irritating, I confess that I've been tempted in that area myself. In meeting a few 'famous' folk myself through the years (I won't mention them here – that would be falling into sin again!), I've found that there's something quite delicious about casually (but rather intentionally) mentioning who I've met. It's a strange way of boasting really and actually is quite silly, as if I become more accomplished or gifted because I've been in the presence of someone accomplished and gifted. Let's face it, all boasting diminishes a person, rather than making them look greater. Boastful people are viewed as insecure braggarts. Surely we boast because we are feeling small and want to inflate our importance in the eyes of others. It's an ugly habit.

As she talks about rejoicing, Hannah uses a term that means, 'to open the mouth wide'. If she's going to shout about anyone, it's going to be about God. That's the right approach to take when we're doing well and when we're either blessed or enjoying a sense of accomplishment. If we're flushed with success and tempted to show off, if I may put it so bluntly (but using the analogy here), let's close our mouths, then open our mouths in thanksgiving to the God who gave us that success in the first place. He really is the only One worth shouting about.

**Prayer: When success comes, keep me humble, Lord. When failure comes, keep me hopeful. Amen.**

# Cheerful giving

Let's remind ourselves of when Hannah sang her beautiful song. Her anthem of praise came when she brought her much-wanted son, Samuel, to Eli the priest and dedicated him to the service of God. This was far more than a moment of ceremony or even thanksgiving. She heads back home but leaves her son behind, entrusted to the priest, surely a heart-rending moment. To wait for years for a child and then to selflessly offer that child into God's service would surely be emotionally traumatic. Not only did she do what she promised, but her song says that she did it joyfully, not with grudging reluctance but with heartfelt praise. She sings her way through her maternal pain.

It's possible to give with a scowl or with regret. Others give but insist that they can control where the money goes and even think that they are buying influence as significant givers. That's not to suggest that designated giving shouldn't be used as directed, or that leaders should not be accountable for the way that church funds are spent. But God loves a cheerful giver (2 Cor. 9:7) – the word means 'hilarious'.

God does not only look at the amount that we give, but the attitude with which we give it. And this doesn't just apply to our giving to church, either. When we serve, listen, randomly bless, are kind, self-sacrificing, or hospitable, we are giving in a variety of different ways. Let's not smear the value of our giving by adopting the wrong attitude as we give.

**Prayer: Lord, help me to be a cheerful giver: of my time, my treasure, my talent. Amen.**

**READ:**
1 Samuel 1:21–28
1 Samuel 2:4–11

**FOCUS**
*'So now I give him to the LORD. For his whole life he shall be given over to the LORD.' (1 Sam. 1:28)*

she did it joyfully … with heartfelt praise

# Songs of fellowship

**READ:**
**Luke 1:39–45**
**Hebrews 10:25**

**FOCUS**
*'In a loud voice she exclaimed: "Blessed are you among women, and blessed is the child you will bear!"' (Luke 1:42)*

Fellowship is a word that provokes images of like-minded people having cups of tea together. Some see fellowship as unnecessary. In a busy life where demands on our time are so high, they ask 'why do we need to gather together for organised church?' Some prefer to occasionally get together with friends to chat, which may or may not include God as a topic. But we are designed to be together. Fellowship has a theological shape in the Bible – it is not something we create as we like in our consumer culture, but is created by God to include prayer, leadership, discipline, sacrament, mission and giving.

Mary's song (which we will be looking at over the next few days) did not flow just as a result of an angel's visit but because God, in His kindness, had given her the opportunity to be with the only other woman on earth who could understand what it felt like to have an angelically announced pregnancy – Elizabeth. These two would have talked about the amazement of being visited by Gabriel; about what it felt like to be used by God in such a mighty way. They would have shared their reflections on the tumultuous happenings that they were caught up in. The relief of being understood, of sharing mutual wonder and experience as well as anxieties and fears, enabled Mary to sing as she did. God has designed us to be together and not just when it's convenient. Songs of joy will be ours when we give ourselves to that togetherness.

**Prayer: Help me, Lord, to sing the song that only comes when it is sung in mutual, committed fellowship. Bless the church where I am blessed to be a part. Amen.**

# Revelation and reflection

As Mary sings her song, so crammed with theology and references to the Old Testament, some insist that a girl of her humble origins could not possibly have come up with such a profound song. But Mary was under the influence of the Holy Spirit, who inspired all Scripture. And as a Jewish girl she would be very familiar with the praise texts of the Old Testament. If her opening words seem familiar, it's because they echo the song of Hannah. As Mary sings about the 'humble state of his servant' she uses the exact same words that are used in the Old Testament by Hannah as she describes her 'misery'. It seems that Mary, initially stunned by the angelic announcement, but then encouraged by her visit to Elizabeth, would have reflected on Hannah's story and used words that flowed from Hannah's heart to describe her own situation. As Mary 'pondered' what she heard, she came to see that she had a massive part in God's big story. Revelation was prompted by reflection and clarity and then joy came too. But that took time and intentionality.

Let's be people who don't rush through Bible reading, just scanning over the words before racing hastily into our day, or breaking speed-reading records when working through a daily Bible reading plan – or even the scriptures linked with these Bible notes. Let's think carefully about the truths that we read, meditate upon the implications of them and allow time to apply them. With all of the distractions we face, that will require discipline.

**Prayer: Father God, I glorify You and rejoice in You, because You are mindful of me. Help me to reflect upon Your truth. Amen.**

**READ:**
**Luke 1:46–48**
**1 Samuel 1:10–11**

**FOCUS**
*'My soul glorifies the Lord and my spirit rejoices in God my Saviour, for he has been mindful of the humble state of his servant.'*
*(Luke 1:46–48)*

under the
influence
of the Holy
Spirit

READ:
Luke 1:46–49 //
1 Peter. 5:5–7

Weekend

# How to be blessed: healthy humility

I mentioned humility earlier. Many of us are confused about what it means to be humble. I meet Christians who think that the only way for them to approach God is with a whining attitude, as they insist that they are useless, worm-like creatures. Others refuse to accept any encouragement, fearing that they might steal some glory from God. But true humility doesn't mean that we deny our gifts, or be continually self-deprecating. Rather, it means that we acknowledge that ultimately whatever we have comes from God. He, as the blesser, is our source. If we are used mightily, we are only channels in His hand.

Mary ponders with amazement the truth that history will call her blessed. Often people from our church tradition refuse to call her the 'blessed virgin Mary', fearing that we are engaging in undue reverence for her. But celebrating Mary's blessedness doesn't mean that we are worshipping her, just honouring her amazing contribution to the kingdom story. Let's acknowledge the source of all that is good in our lives and so walk in a humility that is healthy.

**To ponder: When do you find it difficult to maintain humility?**

whatever we have comes from God

> Even though I now live in London, my family keep sending me copies of your *Every Day with Jesus* Bible reading notes from Nigeria, which encourage me a lot.

## CWR
## Transforming lives through ...

# Worldwide Partnerships

CWR's ministry extends around the globe. Our resources and notes are shipped regularly to Australia and New Zealand, where thousands of free Bible reading notes are also going into prisons each month. Our partner in Nigeria prints and distributes around 100,000 daily devotionals six times a year. We train counsellors in Singapore, provide resources in Malaysia, and will soon be offering teaching in Cambodia. Our resources have been translated into Mandarin, Farsi, Tamil, Sinhala, Korean, Finnish and Welsh – to name but a few! God continues to provide opportunities to cross borders and reach more people every day.

**www.cwr.org.uk/about-cwr**

# God-fearing

**FOCUS**
*'for the Mighty One has done great things for me – holy is his name. His mercy extends to those who fear him'*
*(Luke 1:49–50)*

It's an adjective not frequently used to describe Christians now: God-fearing. As someone who speaks about the heart of the gospel being grace, it's not a term that I'd usually feel comfortable with. I've seen too many Christians who don't enjoy their faith and live in nervous agitation, uncertain about God's heart for them and prone to only come into God's presence with hesitation and even terror. That's not how the Lord wants us to live. The writer to the Hebrews makes it clear that God invites us to draw near to Him with confidence (Heb. 10:22).

But that confidence can become casual and if we're not careful, God becomes just another pal. God is far more than that and when we think of Him just as a 'little' helper we become careless and indifferent about His demands upon our lives. Jesus diminishes into being an adviser rather than Lord.

God is holy. That means that not only is He utterly different from all of creation, pure and without blemish or fault, but for Mary His holiness is demonstrated in His awesome power, enabling a virgin womb to conceive and bringing low and scattering those who oppose Him. Let's also see that as Mary stands amazed at God's awesome holiness, she immediately celebrates God's mercy. Holiness and mercy: both are vital truths about the Lord that we must hold on to. Then our 'fear' of God will be healthy, revering and respecting Him for who He is, yet thrilled by the grace that allows us to know Him as friend as well as Lord.

His holiness is demonstrated in His awesome power

**Prayer: Lord, thank You that You are great, mighty, holy – and merciful. Teach me a healthy reverence for You and Your ways. Amen.**

# A song of justice

READ:
Luke 1:46–56
Matthew 6:33

**FOCUS**
*'He has brought
down rulers from
their thrones but has
lifted up the humble.'*
*(Luke 1:52)*

As we hear Mary talking about God reversing the fortunes of the rich and poor and switching the powerful with the oppressed, we'd be quite wrong to over-spiritualise these statements and just see them in terms of the spiritual work of rescue that is ours in Christ, so that God becomes the rescuer of those who are impoverished because of sin and saves them. The main message of the gospel is not 'get your sins forgiven and go to heaven when you die', but rather 'welcome the kingdom (the rule and reign of God) into your life, become part of His kingdom community (the Church) and become an agent of that kingdom in your everyday life'.

God is passionately concerned about the plight of the poor, the injustices that are done to those under the heel of power brokers in corporations and multinationals, as well as those threatening gangs of thugs who engage in human trafficking. When the King has His way, what is wrong is made right and what is inverted will be put back the right way up. So politics, campaigning for social justice and taking care of the environment are all not just social issues, but kingdom issues.

Let's not back away from our responsibilities and just wait for heaven, but catch a glimpse of what Mary saw and help bring the rule of heaven to earth as we serve, vote and speak out. The gospel is not only about rescue from sin and it's not just about political and social reformation. It's about both.

**Prayer: Lord, as I pray as You have taught us, 'Your kingdom come', help me to live as an agent of Your kingdom rule today. Amen.**

# We know in part

**READ:**
**Luke 1:46–56,**
**67–79**
**1 Corinthians 13:9**

**FOCUS**
*'Praise be to the Lord, the God of Israel, because he has come to his people and redeemed them.'*
*(Luke 1:68)*

Today we're looking at the songs of Mary and Zechariah together. Both sang their songs under the direct anointing of the Holy Spirit – both knew the miraculous power of God, not just in theory but by experience. But both only saw a limited view of what God was doing in the coming of Jesus and John the Baptist.

Mary's song focuses on what the Lord was going to do for Israel, fulfilling the promise given to Abraham; Zechariah picks up a similar theme – the fulfilment of the Abrahamic promises. Both saw that God was doing a remarkable work for Israel, so some have dubbed Mary's words as nationalistic, while Zechariah takes a traditional view of what the Messiah figure would do – overthrow the hated enemies of that nation. Only at the end of Zechariah's song does he begin to grasp that God was coming to rescue Israel from herself, by offering forgiveness. Neither one could begin to fully understand that what they were caught up in would change the world, including the Gentiles. In Zechariah's thinking, God was the God of Israel.

Whatever we know, we don't know it all, because God hasn't given us the keys to unlock every mystery. Mary and Zechariah were granted remarkable insight. But they didn't see the whole picture – perhaps they didn't need to. Let's continue to wrestle with questions, go deeper in our faith and ask God for wisdom. But when answers don't come, let's trust anyway.

**Prayer: I thank You, Father, for the knowledge of salvation, through the forgiveness of sin, because of Your tender mercy, O God. Help me to see what You would have me see. Amen.**

# God knows

It's a technique that Luke often uses in his writings, describing how somebody prophesies about a future event and then pointing to the fulfilment of that prophecy a little later. So it is as Zechariah speaks prophetically about his as yet unborn child, John. Zechariah announces the significant role as prophet that John will have, preparing the way of the Lord. Immediately Luke tells us about the fulfilment of that prophecy. Luke wants us to know that these stupendous events didn't happen by chance, but came about as a result of God's careful planning. Luke's God is not passive, watching from a distance, uninvolved; He dynamically entwines Himself in the unfolding events of human history.

I no longer pray for parking spaces. The Christianity of my earlier years was a faith that insisted God was infinitely involved in every detail of life to a ridiculous level. Neither do I believe that everything is preordained or that everything that happens is the will of God. That's why we are taught to pray that God's kingdom will come and His will be done. God doesn't always get His way. The world is not a puppet theatre with God as the master puppeteer, organising every detail. Nevertheless, we affirm that the overarching purposes of God are going to be fulfilled and that God is able to intervene in the details as we make ourselves available to His purposes daily. Today, we don't have to feel hopeless and abandoned. God will ultimately have His will and way with this planet. The big plan will be fulfilled.

**Prayer: You are working to a huge plan, Lord. Help me today to take my place in that plan. Amen.**

**READ:**
**Luke 1:67–79**
**Matthew 6:9–13**

**FOCUS**
*'And you, my child, will be called a prophet of the Most High; for you will go on before the Lord to prepare the way for him' (Luke 1:76)*

God will ultimately have His will and way

# Angels and peace

READ:
**Luke 2:1–14**
**Isaiah 9:1–7**

**FOCUS**
*'Glory to God in the highest heaven, and on earth peace to those on whom his favour rests.'*
*(Luke 2:14)*

Peace is a concept that we Christians tend to minimise. Often we talk about peace in merely emotional, subjective terms: when thinking about guidance, believers frequently say that they 'feel peace' about their decision. To have peace is seen as the experience of inner calm, perhaps in chaotic and turbulent circumstances. Of course, a sense of inner harmony is hugely important and is a part of all that Christ offers as we come to Him: He is the Jesus who says 'Don't let your hearts be troubled'.

But for Jewish people, the concept of peace is much bigger than just emotional equilibrium. The greeting 'shalom' is a pregnant word loaded with significance. Shalom speaks of being at peace with God, with one's neighbour, with the environment, as well as within oneself. It is holistic health, but also speaks of political and social harmony. That's why the angels couldn't resist bursting into song, because when people truly follow Jesus, peace results. If our world could learn to live self-sacrificially, to know blessing through meekness, to be preoccupied with giving rather than grabbing, then while it would never be perfect, it would be a much better place as gradually the kingdom of God is established. A world that operates in the way that the Creator designed it to operate would obviously be a much better place.

Total peace will never be established until the kingdom comes in fullness when Christ returns, but in the meantime, the kingdom can advance slowly and gradually – and that can happen today.

**Prayer: Make me a channel of Your kingdom peace, Jesus, Prince of Peace. Amen.**

peace is much bigger than just emotional equilibrium

> The rooms are airy and spacious. The whole place has a peaceful and accommodating feel – a delightful venue.

**CWR**

Transforming lives through ...

# Magnificent Venues

Every day, the CWR team has the privilege of working in historic buildings and beautiful surroundings. The spacious, characterful rooms and grounds can be hired for a church, business or private function, including overnight accommodation, if required. Come and experience the peaceful atmosphere and enjoy the unique surroundings offered at either Waverley Abbey House in Surrey or Pilgrim Hall in East Sussex.

**www.waverleyabbeyhouse.org.uk**
**www.pilgrimhall.com**

READ:
Luke 2:25–32

Weekend

# Mind the gap

As I write this, I'm travelling on the last train from London. I managed to get somewhat lost on the Underground system. But what rings in my mind tonight is the monotone voice warning us to 'mind the gap' between the platform and the train. People of faith have to learn to mind the gap – the gap between the promises of God and the fulfilment of those promises. Simeon, an elderly man, had been assured that he would not die before he saw the Messiah. Luke doesn't tell us how Simeon received that pledge from God, only that he received it. But as someone who, together with the rest of Israel, was living under the heel of Roman oppression, Simeon had waited, perhaps for years, for the promised Messiah to appear. Perhaps he'd wandered around the Temple every morning, looking for a child who might be the One, hoping that the Holy Spirit would confirm the identity of that child. And now, at last, Jesus was here. The waiting was over and now Simeon could sing his song and die in peace.

It's wonderful when God speaks, when He breaks into a deadlocked, hopeless situation and brings a promise of future blessing. But when that happens, we will need to learn to hang in there, to endure, to mind the gap and to continue to trust when the promise seems to be forgotten and the answer we long for seems like it will never arrive. If you're waiting in that gap, may you know grace to strengthen you in the waiting.

**To ponder: What does it mean to you to wait 'in the gap'?**

God ... brings a promise of future blessing

# Remember what God has said

**READ:**
Luke 2:25–32
Matthew 28:19

**FOCUS**
*'For my eyes have seen your salvation, which you have prepared in the sight of all nations: a light for revelation to the Gentiles, and the glory of your people Israel.'
(Luke 2:30–32)*

We've already seen that Mary and Zechariah had wonderful but limited revelation as they sang their songs, seeing the Messiah as coming primarily as the rescuer of Israel. It's elderly Simeon who clearly declares the truth that Jesus is coming as a light to the Gentiles. He is not only the Saviour of Israel, but is the One who comes to save the whole world. This announcement about His mission to the Gentiles was made early in Jesus' life. Thirty-three years later, before ascending to the Father, Jesus clearly told His disciples to take the kingdom message into 'all the world'. But for decades the Early Church struggled to grasp the breadth of the mission and in the end, Gentiles began flooding into the Church, not because of the strategic planning of the then headquarters church in Jerusalem, but through the organic, spontaneous witness of the scattered exiles from Jerusalem.

But old Simeon had sung about Gentile inclusion right from the time Jesus was a baby.

Let's take note of what we learn in life and not only record and remember what God has said to us in our journeys, but make sure that we are living in the light of His words as we walk in obedience. Failure to do that will mean that we live a frustrating life, going around in endless circles, forced to relearn the same old lessons repeatedly. Are some of us heading in a direction that we know is clearly wrong, but are stubbornly trudging along anyway, insisting that our own way is better?

**Prayer: Help me, Lord, to remember, apply and stay faithful to what You have already told me. Amen.**

# When the past is better

**READ:**
**Psalm 77:1–20**
**Lamentations 3:22–25**

**FOCUS**
*'I thought about the former days, the years of long ago'*
*(Psa. 77:5)*

Earlier I was looking at a holiday picture of our children, who were young teenagers at the time. We're covered in dust and the smiles on our grubby faces are broad. It was a beautiful day – one that won't ever be repeated in quite the same way. For just a moment, I hankered for that season in our lives. I wanted to go back. I can't.

The singer of this song is in despair as he ponders the past. He's crying out to God continually, but without consolation. It's not that there's regret in the past, but rather he pines for what used to be. So low does he feel, he even expresses his deep doubts in the goodness and consistency of God to be able to keep His promises.

When we battle doubt or feel angry with God, we don't need to try to hide those feelings from Him, but they can form part of our prayer. God knows our hearts anyway and is looking for authenticity, not superficial speeches.

Helpfully, anguished Asaph turns a corner in this song of his and comes to see that the past was a blessing to be celebrated, but not a season to try to recreate.

Perhaps you're looking back on better days. It could be that very real tragedy has shattered your life and your memories are bitter sweet. May you be strengthened to be able to remember and know comfort and joy as you do so, even in the midst of pain. You can't go back, I know. But may you know strength today.

God knows our hearts

**Prayer: Whatever was, help me to know You and live for You today, Lord. Amen.**

# I didn't do it my way

The vintage chart topper for funerals is still *My Way* by Frank Sinatra. But *My Way* is not the song of the redeemed, because we're not called to celebrate independence, but rather dependency upon God. We were not created to stand on our own two feet, but rather walk in a relationship with the God who wants to guide and help us. This is not a confession of weakness, but simply an acknowledgement that we want to live as the Creator intended.

Tomorrow we're going to look at another victory song, this time sung by King Jehoshaphat and his army. But it's worth pausing to look at the prayer that preceded the song, found in 2 Chronicles, chapter 20, verse 12.

Let's look at a bit of background information. Judah was under attack from an army whose identity is not mentioned. What we do know is that it was vast – so huge, that the king was alarmed. But fear drove him not into blind terror, but vibrant trust as he called a national fast and then prayed one of the most powerful, simple prayers: 'We do not know what to do, but our eyes are on you.'

What a relief to know that not only are we not alone, left to our own 'ingenious' devices, but that God is with us, for us, interested in us. Let's not drift into a 'My Way' mentality. If we're deliberately stomping our feet, with our fingers figuratively in our ears, let's come back quickly and choose *Amazing Grace*, or something similar, as our theme song. It's a much better song selection.

**Prayer: God, be my power, my wisdom, my strength and then, my song. Amen.**

**READ:**
**2 Chronicles 20:1–12**
**Isaiah 55:8–9**

**FOCUS**
*'For we have no power to face this vast army that is attacking us. We do not know what to do, but our eyes are on you.' (2 Chron. 20:12)*

# Sing it loud

READ:
2 Chronicles
20:13–19
Psalm 47:1-9

**FOCUS**
*'Then some Levites
from the Kohathites
and Korahites stood
up and praised the
LORD, the God of
Israel, with a very
loud voice.'*
(2 Chron. 20:19)

Tomorrow we'll look briefly at the song that the army of Judah sang on the battlefield. But before we do, let's just take note that before the battle began the Levitical priests got musical and turned the volume up. Energy and volume were important as the troops prepared for the fight of their lives – but one that God was going to fight for them. It must have seemed quite mad to send a choir out onto the battlefield – and somewhat terrifying for the choir too. One would feel vulnerable if one was armed with nothing more than a tambourine. Appointing a choir seemed like a strange military strategy – but it was a strategy that brought success.

Sometimes the thought of singing songs for 20 minutes (or, for some of us, an hour or more!) isn't attractive. And there's a tendency in some of the larger churches around the world for worship to become more of a performance, with the congregation watching rather than singing. I think that's a dangerous trend – worship is about participation, not being a spectator. But when I sing and sing loudly, despite my feelings or circumstances, I can realign my heart, soul and mind with the lyrics that I'm singing. Worship and warfare are linked. Let's not be casual about gathering for worship – personal wars can be won or lost as a result. And when our singing lacks enthusiasm, gathering for worship becomes a dull trial rather than an inspirational time of refuelling. Even if you don't have an angelic voice (I don't), sing it loud!

**Prayer: Help me, Lord, to worship You with passion, energy and sacrifice. Amen.**

# What to sing when life is impossible

**READ:**
**2 Chronicles**
**20:20–30**

**FOCUS**
*'Jehoshaphat appointed men to sing to the LORD and to praise him for the splendour of his holiness as they went out at the head of the army, saying: "Give thanks to the LORD, for his love endures for ever."'*
*(2 Chron. 20:21)*

It's reported that a world-renowned theologian was asked by a member of the press what his greatest theological insight and discovery was. The answer came as a surprise. His reply: 'Jesus loves me – this I know, for the Bible tells me so.' The words of a children's song summarised his most profound discovery to date: Jesus loved him.

When the army of Judah found itself trembling with fear in the face of impossible odds, they sang a song about the enduring love of God – and they gave thanks for that love, a theme that was picked up in the psalm that we considered earlier.

When life is impossible, we can feel like there is so much that we don't know or understand. When and how will this season of tears end? Is God going to intervene? What is His wisdom for us as we are faced with a myriad of decisions? What is to become of us?

Whatever the circumstances, we are loved. We are not alone, abandoned or uncared for. And that, amazingly, can nudge us into singing a song of thanksgiving even on the fiercest battlefield. We don't give thanks for the war or pretend that we are grateful for the threat or the pain, but we can give thanks for the promise of love when other loves have faded or failed us. And as we sing our song, we catch a hint of victory and strength, even as Jehoshaphat and his army did so many centuries ago.

Praising on the battlefield – it seems crazy. But then following God frequently does.

**Prayer: Strengthen weary warriors on the battlefield of life, Lord. Give them a new song today. Amen.**

We are not alone, abandoned or uncared for

# A SPECIAL VISIT TO ISRAEL
## WITH JEFF AND KAY LUCAS

**In 2017, Kay and I are off to the Holy Land, and we'd like to invite you to come along with us!**

We'll be taking in some of the wonderful, inspiring sights of Jerusalem, and enjoying the simple beauty of Galilee. We'll be visiting some key biblical locations, starting in Upper Galilee and the Jordan Valley. We'll drive through the Hula Valley and along the Eastern Shore of Galilee, with a stop at Bethsaida, before passing Jericho and ascending to Jerusalem. We'll go south to the Ashkelon area, which will include a visit to Nahal Sorek, where Samson had his hair cut. We will visit what was biblical Gath and the site most closely associated with Samson at Tell es-Safi. No visit to Jerusalem would be complete without a stop at the Western (Wailing) Wall and the Temple Mount, St Stephen's Gate, the Pool of Bethesda and the Via Dolorosa. A day walking in the City of God concludes with evening worship.

The next day, starting from the Mount of Olives, we'll visit Dominus Flevit, the Garden of Gethsemane and the Garden Tomb, where there will be an opportunity for shared Communion led by Kay. In the afternoon, we'll visit Bethlehem and view the Church of the Nativity and the Shepherd's Fields. We'll travel down the Jericho Road to the lowest point on earth at approximately 1,300 feet below sea level, enjoy a visit to Qumran where the Dead Sea Scrolls were found, and then ascend to the summit of Masada by cable car to hear its amazing story. Last, we visit the Israel Museum to see the Dead Sea Scrolls and the amazing Holyland Model of Jerusalem, showing the city as it may well have been in the time of Jesus, before a final visit to the Old City for some haggling or simple relaxation. Kay and I would be delighted to have you with us.

*Truly a trip of a lifetime, I highly recommend a journey to the Holy Land with Jeff and Kay Lucas. Not only was the experience so inspiring and memorable, but the tour was handled with such great attention to detail, with knowledgeable guides and top accommodation.*

Karen Bauer, (2014 trip)

**For booking details call Chris on 01938 561604 or email chris@travelinkuk.com**

## An erotic song

I know, you're probably a little shocked by the title that I've given today's reflection. But my choice of words is intentional. We tend to think of the word 'erotic' in negative terms. It's a word that's been stolen by the porn industry that enslaves millions and makes billions. But God created the erotic and it's important to note that a lengthy song celebrating human sexuality is found in Scripture. And even though Solomon was a prolific songwriter, he considered that song the best he'd composed, out of all 1,005 songs he penned in total (1 Kings 4:32). He called that erotic song about faithful sexual love his 'song of songs' (Songs 1:1). It's a song of praise – for sex.

Throughout history, the Church has shied away from celebrating sex. In some churches, wholesome teaching on sex is frowned on – one of the few times that someone loudly marched out during my preaching was during a talk on that subject. And there are worrying statistics about how Christians approach sex before marriage and marriage itself. But our sexuality is a gift to be valued, celebrated and expressed in the way that God intended.

**To ponder: Why has the Church often been nervous about sex, often celebrating lifelong abstinence as the spiritual ideal?**

sexuality is a gift to be valued

# Jailhouse rock

READ:
Acts 16:16–40
Psalm 20:1–9

**FOCUS**
*'About midnight Paul and Silas were praying and singing hymns to God, and the other prisoners were listening to them.' (Acts 16:25)*

It's hard to sing when you're really hurting and after the very severe beating that Paul and Silas would have suffered in the Philippian jail, they found themselves not only with terrible wounds but in an impossible bind – literally.

Notice how Luke tells us that the pair were incarcerated in 'an inner cell, their feet fastened with stocks'. They couldn't even lie down without discomfort. But while you can put shackles on a believer, you can't cage their soul. Paul and Silas launched into praise at midnight. The hour was dark, their lacerated backs hurt and the future was bleak, but they sang. We're not told what they sang, only that their songs were directed to God. And then while Luke doesn't reveal the lyrics, he does record an interesting response from the other prisoners – they were listening.

When God enables us to sing in the midst of suffering, the world sits up and takes notice. Many readers will know of the singer Ishmael. Ishmael is a close friend and I watched somewhat helplessly as he walked through leukaemia some years ago. But his quiet kindness in the hospital and his tenacious trust in God made such an impact on those around and continue to do so. Now he serves as a hospital chaplain on the very same ward where he received treatment.

God doesn't make us suffer so that we can sing and be overheard. But when we suffer well and sing in the darkness, others may well listen in and be amazed.

**Prayer: Lord, when it is midnight in my life and all seems dark, help me to sing. And may others listen and even join in with the song. Amen.**

# Sing, whatever the weather

**READ:**
**James 5:13**
**1 Thessalonians**
**5:17–18**

**FOCUS**
*'Is anyone among you in trouble? Let them pray. Is anyone happy? Let them sing songs of praise.'*
*(James 5:13)*

Yesterday we witnessed two faithful servants of Jesus singing their hearts out in prison. We might think it's harder to sing when you're in trouble, but perhaps that's when we're most likely to lift our voices because we urgently need God's help. As we saw earlier in our journey through some of the songs of the Bible, success can be dangerous, not only making us headstrong, but when life is easy we can drift away from dependency on the Lord. James addresses that tendency, calling us to sing whatever the season in our lives. So we're commanded to pray when in trouble and sing when we're happy – in other words, whichever extremity we find ourselves in, whether life is a struggle or a delight, come to God anyway, faithful in every unfolding chapter of life. One writer puts it like this, 'James commands that Christians pray throughout the whole spectrum of emotions. Whether low or high, at the bottom or the top, in the pits or on the pinnacle, either prayer or praise is appropriate.'*

James offers us a simple choice and doesn't make the options of indifference, faithless anger, or empty despair available. When it's sunny, be sure to sing. When the clouds roll in and life is endlessly overcast, pray. And the word that James uses has the meaning of 'continually' in it. Choose now. And do it. Always.

I know, it sounds too simple. But I'd like to live by James' instruction and pray or sing my way through all that is yet to come.

**Prayer: Lord, whatever the season, help me sing, pray, or both. Amen.**

*\*R. Kent Hughes, James: Faith that Works (Wheaton, Illinois: Crossway Books, 1991) p124*

when life is easy we can drift away from dependency

# Sing the truth

READ:
**Colossians 3:1–17**
**Psalm 47:7**

W e're not called to sing solos in the kingdom. Being part of the Church, the family of God, is not just vital for our own spiritual development. God's plan is nothing less than the reaching of planet Earth through communities of redemption. Frankly, if Church did nothing for us (which is highly unlikely, seeing it is part of God's strategy), then we'd still need to be part of Church. As Paul calls his friends in Colossae to make sung worship a priority because it enables them to constantly receive the message of Christ, we see this principle: the words that we sing matter because they shape our theology, and our theology shapes our view of the world, of ourselves and most importantly, our view of God.

**FOCUS**
*'Let the message of Christ dwell among you richly as you teach and admonish one another with all wisdom through psalms, hymns, and songs from the Spirit' (Col. 3:16)*

Commentators have argued for centuries about what Paul means when he talks about 'psalms, hymns and songs from the Spirit'. Defining the first two is obvious, but are 'songs from the Spirit' spontaneous compositions of exhortation or praises to God? I was once part of a church where people would spontaneously get up and sing about God, inviting the worship band to follow them as they did and the result was beautiful and remarkable. Whether Paul was referring to this is uncertain; what is clear is that what we sing matters. I'm not one of those heresy hunters who are constantly looking for any theological flaws in worship songs, but I do think that we should think carefully about what we sing. After all, aren't we singing it because we believe it to be true?

**Prayer: I want to grow in my knowledge of You, Lord. Thank You for the way that sung worship can contribute to that growth. Amen.**

# From the heart

**READ:**
**Colossians 3:1–17**
**Psalm 103:1**

**FOCUS**
*'singing to God with gratitude in your hearts.'* (Col. 3:16)

'Put your heart into it.' It's a phrase we use to encourage commitment, effort and full engagement in what might be a difficult task. When we talk about something that is 'heartfelt', we're saying that we feel deeply about it.

Let's read Paul's encouragement to the Colossians again, because I don't want us to miss the place of the heart in his words. He encourages us not just to sing songs of truth that will 'teach and admonish with all wisdom', but to have gratitude to God in our hearts as we sing. And that challenges me.

Sometimes I catch myself mechanically singing songs, going through the motions of worship. My lips are moving but my heart is not in it and I am not fully present in the act of praise – I'm singing songs about God, ostensibly to God, but my mind is really somewhere else. But then as I sit here tapping away at 5am (we have a noisy owl living in our porch who has been greeting us far too early in the day), I'm challenged to fully 'put my heart' into living out my faith today. Notice that Paul moves quickly from worship to wider lifestyle, calling the Colossians to do *everything* 'in the name of the Lord Jesus, giving thanks to God the Father through him'.

Today promises to be busy. But I don't want it to pass in a blur of activity, surviving it, getting the necessary tasks done, without there being heartfelt worship, commitment and conversation with God. Let's put our hearts into today.

**Prayer: Lord, You have my heart. Help me to consciously walk with You today, so that my day becomes an act of worship in all that I do. Amen.**

# A call to worship

READ:
**Ephesians 5:1–20**
**Psalm 95:1–11**

**FOCUS**
*'be filled with the Spirit, speaking to one another with psalms, hymns, and songs from the Spirit. Sing and make music from your heart to the Lord' (Eph. 5:18–19)*

It's sometimes said that worship is for God, not for us. But that's not entirely true. As we sing our songs there's a sense in which we sing to each other as well as to the Lord. Our worship is a call to one another to bring praise. Just as the psalmist includes mutual exhortation as well as words of adoration, 'Come, let us sing for joy to the LORD, let us shout aloud to the Rock of our salvation ... Come, let us bow down in worship' (Psa. 95:1,6), so as we gather, we offer an invitation to each other to bless the Lord.

The practice of singing to and with each other has long been part of the Church. Roman governor Pliny remarked how the Christians that he knew had the custom of meeting on a fixed day before dawn and 'reciting a hymn antiphonally to Christ as God'.

Consider the implications of this for a moment. We won't always immediately feel able to engage in worship; a heart alignment will often be needed and we can help each other to draw near to God. As the choir launches into their first piece, as the worship band kicks into gear or the organist touches the keys and as we begin to express words of truth, our hearts are warmed.

Yesterday I talked about wanting to put my whole heart into worship and live a worshipful life. But that won't happen automatically. It will come from discipline, silence, intentional reflection, meditation on Scripture, fasting, prayer and, yes, diligent commitment to shared worship as well.

**Prayer: Lord, when my heart is cold or heavy, help me to offer and heed the call to worship. Amen.**

worship is a call to one another to bring praise

# What are we bringing?

READ:
1 Corinthians
14:26 //
Ephesians 5:19

It was a wonderful but rather dangerous practice that we called 'open worship'. Prior to sharing Communion, the church I was a part of would spend 20–30 minutes during which anyone could pray, read a scripture, exercise one of the gifts of the Spirit, or – and here comes the dangerous part – launch into a worship song which would (hopefully) result in the whole congregation joining in. The challenge was twofold: sometimes the congregation didn't know the selected song (leading to a rather awkward solo) but the more regular difficulty was that the person who had launched into song pitched it in entirely the wrong key, leading to an unfortunate but hilarious time of high-pitched congregational shrieking. But if 'open worship' was occasionally awkward, it was certainly beautiful, because there was such a sense of contribution and participation.

Perhaps something like this is what Paul points to when he refers to the gathering of the Corinthians as he says, 'each of you has a … hymn'. I know we touched on this earlier, but it's worth repeating: whatever our style of worship, let's participate.

**To ponder: What does participation in worship mean?**

whatever our style of
worship, let's participate

# A song that spurred jealousy

Reading some stories from a well-known author, I was moved by his confession that, as a pastor, he used to like having visiting speakers come into his church and do well, as long as they didn't do too well. His honesty caused me to respect him more. While competitiveness and jealousy, much of it fuelled by insecurity, can strike us all, I was glad he admitted to occasional struggles in this area.

Comparing yourself with others is a bad idea, whether it's about looks, talents, wealth, influence or anything else. It's futile and self-destructive to live with envy. That was one of the causes of Saul's downfall. He had to be the top dog. Having said that, he was placed in a very difficult position. Some songs in the Bible were well intentioned, but unwise. One example of that is the song composed after David had repeatedly been successful on the battlefield. The song became so popular that even the enemy knew it. Imagine Saul's predicament: he was the reigning king but had not been able to do anything about the threat of the loud Philistine, Goliath. And now a previously unknown shepherd boy, David, was being celebrated not only as a national hero, but with greater adulation than Saul, who had killed thousands, according to the refrain, but David had killed tens of thousands. It might have been wiser to keep both men out of the song and just give thanks to God for national deliverance.

When everyone is singing the praises of others and you feel overlooked, be careful to guard your heart.

**READ:**
1 Samuel 18:1–9
James 3:14–15

**FOCUS**
*'Saul has slain his thousands, and David his tens of thousands.'*
(1 Sam. 18:7)

**Prayer: Lord, help me to be content with who You have called me to be. Deliver me from the tyranny of comparison with others. Amen.**

# The right hand of God

**READ:**
**Psalm 60:1–8**
**Luke 10:17–20**

**FOCUS**
*'Save us and help us
with your right hand,
that those you love
may be delivered.'*
(Psa. 60:5)

In Scripture, 'God's right hand' is a metaphor for God's favour and blessing. David speaks of it here and Jesus is described as sitting at the right hand of the Father.

I remember being invited as a guest preacher one time and nobody in the church knew about the theme I had chosen. Just a minute or so before getting up to preach, Linda, one of the leaders there and a friend, walked across to me. Imagine my amazement when she simply asked me to extend my right hand and then took oil used to anoint people for prayer and poured it onto my hands. Without any further words, she smiled and walked away. I could hardly believe it as I stood up to preach on the right hand of favour, with my own hand dripping with oil used to ask for blessing! God was making me aware of His love and grace towards me – a heart that is expressed in this psalm for all of God's people, as David speaks of those who God loves being 'delivered'. The Hebrew word used here really belongs in a love poem, so rich and tender is the word used.

In the midst of his successes, mingled with some failures, David celebrated that he was favoured by God. Jesus warned His friends and disciples not to be primarily focused on ministry successes and even their authority over demons, but rather to be delighted because their names were written in heaven – they are loved by God and belong to Him, just as we are loved by God and belong to Him. Whatever we don't know today, we can know that we are loved and favoured.

**Prayer: Thank You for Your love, for Your salvation, for Your rescue and for Your favour, Lord. Amen.**

we are loved
and favoured

# NEXT ISSUE

## Heart strings  **MAR/APR 2016**

Having taken a look at some of the songs throughout
the Bible, next month we are going to focus on
some of the Psalms that flowed from the heart and
pen of David, and endeavour to line them up with
episodes from his life. This enables us not only to
learn from his history, but ponder his responses and
reactions to seasons of joy, hardship, questioning,
failure and pain. The Bible offers us instruction
for the whole of life, not just the sunnier days. And
David, walking with God as he did thousands of
years ago, can teach us how to navigate our own
journeys. Join me and share in this fascinating study.

Obtain your
copy from CWR
or a Christian
bookshop

**Also available as eBook/eSubscription**

# Dependency upon God

**READ:**
**Psalm 60:1–12**
**John 15:1–17**

**FOCUS**
*'With God we shall gain the victory, and he will trample down our enemies.'*
(Psa. 60:12)

At a leaders' conference I was called up to the platform and presented with a bishop's staff. I was told to carry the staff whenever in a ministry situation – some readers might remember me trudging around Spring Harvest with it slung over my shoulder. The whole thing seemed faintly ridiculous and was not only quite intrusive (a lapel pin would have been easier to carry than a lengthy wooden staff!) but potentially caused some misunderstandings. Was I just a weirdo or an attention seeker? Was carrying a bishop's staff somewhat pretentious for a young man who was not remotely a bishop?

But the key truth behind this strange action was found in the prophecy given that night, 'Carry it as a sign of dependency, to remind you where your strength comes from. It comes from God.' I'm convinced that the 'sign' was primarily for me, not for others – as someone who can be impulsive and independent, the staff daily reminded me that without Christ I can do nothing of enduring worth. David acknowledges that vital truth in his psalm as he pictures a mighty God parcelling out land as He pleases and tossing His shoe over Edom like a man flinging his shoe into a corner at the end of a busy day. David doesn't presume upon God's help, but makes a specific request for it. God is our helper. Ask for His help and strength today. And if you're wondering why these strange things don't happen to you, perhaps you don't need them to bolster your faith or restrain a tendency to independence.

Ask for His help and strength today

**Prayer: Mighty God, give us aid against the enemy, for human help is worthless. My strength comes from You, Lord. Amen.**

# A song for success

How quickly we forget that success can be dangerous. We can be the most vulnerable when we are feeling strong. And accomplishment can cause us to be blinded to areas in our lives where we are not doing so well.

David was riding high at this time in his reign as king. He had just won a tremendous battle against the Syrians (2 Sam. 8:13) and was extremely popular as a result. But all was not entirely well because there is sadness in the midst of success, as David cries out to God in lament. We're not entirely sure what had gone wrong. Some believe that King David was grieving over a previous, unsuccessful campaign against his enemies, which would have cost many lives, before a final, decisive victory was won. Others think that while David and his army were engaged in warfare far away from home, a neighbouring nation had taken the opportunity to mount an attack. Whatever was wrong, David was not blind to it and saw the defeat as an expression of the judgment of God. Now he calls on the Lord to allow the 'banner to be unfurled' – a request for blessing so that God's people could once again live as a banner, a sign to the nations around them, as they lived faithfully for and with God.

Let's watch when we stand, lest we fall, as Paul warns. When we become aware of our strengths because of success, let's remember that blessing comes from God and continue to be grateful for strength, but fully aware of our weaknesses.

**Prayer: Restore me now, Lord, and keep me close, especially when I feel strong and successful. Amen.**

**READ:**
Psalm 60:1–4
1 Corinthians 10:12

**FOCUS**
*'You have rejected us, God, and burst upon us; you have been angry – now restore us!'*
(Psa. 60:1)

# Singing is better than griping

**READ:**
**Numbers 21:16–20**
**Exodus 17:1–4**

**FOCUS**
*'Spring up, O well!*
*Sing about it,*
*about the well that*
*the princes dug,*
*that the nobles of*
*the people sank*
*– the nobles with*
*sceptres and staffs.'*
*(Num. 21:17–18)*

Victor Meldrew is the ever-complaining misery from *One Foot in the Grave*, his catchphrase was 'I don't believe it!' Victor saw life as a hunt for opportunities to complain. Recently I spent some time in the company of a real-life Victor. He griped about the food we were eating, the weather, the driver in front, the traffic in general – after a while, it became almost amusing. Living a life of relative ease and comfort, the poor chap was determined to complain at every opportunity.

Israel did something similar, bringing Moses to the brink of despair with their incessant whinging. The complaining reached fever pitch when they got concerned about water supplies, which was a very real problem in such an arid part of the world. Fear is often the trigger for complaint.

But on this occasion in Numbers, perhaps chastened by the judgment that God had brought upon them for their murmuring, they cancelled their complaining and sang instead. As they sang, they were surprised to discover a well where they least expected it.

In writing this note today, I'm challenged that I can be a real-life Victor at times; bristling at minor irritations, I murmur with discontent rather than celebrate what is good. And when that becomes my habit, 'I don't believe it' becomes my mantra too – a complaining heart can easily become a faithless heart. I don't want to live that way today and perhaps if we sing rather than moan, we might be more likely to be surprised by the goodness of God.

**Prayer: Help me to see the well rather than the wilderness, Lord. Amen.**

# The final exodus

READ:
Exodus 15:1–18 //
Revelation 15:1–4

The book of Revelation has been interpreted in many weird and wonderful ways, but at its heart is this message: Jesus wins. His victory is secure forever. And because we are in Him, we win too. All of this is possible because, against all odds, we have been rescued. John clearly wants us to connect the end of time with that event that is so central in Jewish history – the Exodus. Remember? The people were helpless, powerless against the might of the Egyptians. But God led them out in victory. Now, as John describes the 'song of Moses and the lamb', he connects that great Exodus event with the Lamb of God, Jesus. We're in the new exodus, marching into eternity with Christ.

Perhaps today there's a Red Sea in front of you and there's no way ahead, or so it seems. I don't know if it will part but this much is certain: one day every challenge will be banished, every threat will fade and every tear will be wiped away as Jesus leads us on into eternity. May your heart and mind be strengthened in that knowledge today.

**To ponder: What is your 'Red Sea'?**

Jesus wins. His victory is secure forever

# Revelation song

**READ:**
**Revelation 5:1–14**
**1 Peter 2:4–10**

**FOCUS**
*'You have made them to be a kingdom and priests to serve our God, and they will reign on the earth.' (Rev. 5:10)*

The song of the Lamb, the song that will be sung to Jesus, the only One worthy of such a planet-wide, universal celebration, is surely the greatest in human history. He is the Lamb, the One who willingly gave Himself for us, holding nothing back, such is His love. But then notice a theme that is in that song, one that Peter picks up on in his letter – He has made us to be a kingdom and priests, people from every part of the globe and one day we will reign with Him. This is our song: we are not self-made people, but people rescued through the cross, redeemed from being enemies of God and now found at the very centre of His eternal purposes. He alone has accomplished this. And if our salvation is the fruit of His work, He will continue to make and shape us into all that He wants us to be – He has begun the work and He will finish it (Phil. 1:6).

As we conclude, allow me to do something I've never done before. Just recently I discovered a video from a worship concert that stirred my heart and moved me to tears of gratitude. Why not take eight minutes of your time and tune in to that beautiful song from Revelation 5? Search 'Kari Jobe Revelation Song' on YouTube or another online video site. And know this. There are many songs that are based on fiction, the fruit of creative imagination. But the song of the Lamb, the song of the triumphant Jesus – that song is true.

we are ... people rescued through the cross

**Prayer: Lord Jesus, You are worthy of honour and glory and praise, now, this day and forever. Amen.**

# ORDER FORM

## 5 EASY WAYS TO ORDER:

1. Phone in your credit card order: **01252 784700** (Mon–Fri, 9.30am – 5pm)
2. Visit our online store at **www.cwr.org.uk/store**
3. Send this form together with your payment to:
   **CWR, Waverley Abbey House, Waverley Lane, Farnham, Surrey GU9 8EP**
4. Visit a Christian bookshop
5. For Australia and New Zealand visit KI Entertainment at **www.cwr4u.net.au**

For a list of our National Distributors, who supply countries outside the UK, visit www.cwr.org.uk/distributors

## YOUR DETAILS (REQUIRED FOR ORDERS AND DONATIONS)

| | |
|---|---|
| **Full Name:** | **CWR ID No.** (if known): |
| **Home Address:** | |
| | **Postcode:** |
| **Telephone No.** (for queries): | **Email:** |

## PUBLICATIONS

| TITLE | QTY | PRICE | TOTAL |
|---|---|---|---|
| | | | |
| | | | |
| | | | |
| | | | |
| | | | |
| | | **Total publications** | |

All CWR adult Bible-reading notes are also available in eBook and email subscription format.
Visit www.cwr.org.uk for further information.

**UK p&p:** up to £24.99 = **£2.99**; £25.00 and over = **FREE**

**Elsewhere p&p:** up to £10 = **£4.95**; £10.01 - £50 = **£6.95**; £50.01 - £99.99 = **£10**; £100 and over = **£30**

Please allow 14 days for delivery — Total publications and p&p **A**

## SUBSCRIPTIONS* (NON DIRECT DEBIT)

| | QTY | PRICE (INCLUDING P&P) | | | TOTAL |
|---|---|---|---|---|---|
| | | UK | Europe | Elsewhere | |
| *Every Day with Jesus* (1yr, 6 issues) | | £15.95 | £19.95 | Please contact nearest National Distributor or CWR direct | |
| Large Print *Every Day with Jesus* (1yr, 6 issues) | | £15.95 | £19.95 | | |
| *Inspiring Women Every Day* (1yr, 6 issues) | | £15.95 | £19.95 | | |
| *Life Every Day* (Jeff Lucas) (1yr, 6 issues) | | £15.95 | £19.95 | | |
| *Mettle*: 14-18s (1yr, 3 issues) | | £14.50 | £16.60 | | |
| *YP's*: 11-15s (1yr, 6 issues) | | £15.95 | £19.95 | | |
| *Topz*: 7-11s (1yr, 6 issues) | | £15.95 | £19.95 | | |
| *Cover to Cover Every Day* (1yr, 6 issues) | | Email subscription only, to order visit online store. | | | |
| **Total Subscriptions** (Subscription prices already include postage and packing) **B** | | | | | |

Please circle which bimonthly issue you would like your subscription to commence from:

**JAN/FEB MAR/APR MAY/JUN JUL/AUG SEP/OCT NOV/DEC**

\* Only use this section for subscriptions paid for by credit/debit card or
cheque. For Direct Debit subscriptions see overleaf.

**CONTINUED OVERLEAF >>**

<< SEE PREVIOUS PAGE FOR START OF ORDER FORM

## PAYMENT DETAILS

☐ I enclose a cheque/PO made payable to CWR for the amount of: £ _____

☐ Please charge my credit/debit card.

**Cardholder's Name** (in BLOCK CAPITALS) _____

Card No. ☐☐☐☐ ☐☐☐☐ ☐☐☐☐ ☐☐☐☐

Expires End ☐☐☐☐         Security Code ☐☐☐

**GIFT TO CWR** ☐ Please send me an acknowledgement of my gift     **C** ☐

## GIFT AID (YOUR HOME ADDRESS REQUIRED, SEE OVERLEAF)

*giftaid it*   I am a UK taxpayer and want CWR to reclaim the tax on all my donations for the four years prior to this year **and on** all donations I make from the date of this Gift Aid declaration until further notice.*

**Taxpayer's Full Name** (in BLOCK CAPITALS) _____

**Signature** _____     **Date** _____

*I understand I must pay an amount of Income/Capital Gains Tax at least equal to the tax the charity reclaims in the tax year.

**GRAND TOTAL** (Total of A, B, & C) ☐

## SUBSCRIPTIONS BY DIRECT DEBIT (UK BANK ACCOUNT HOLDERS ONLY)

Subscriptions cost £15.95 (except *Mettle*: £14.50) for one year for delivery within the UK. Please tick relevant boxes and fill in the form be

☐ *Every Day with Jesus* (1yr, 6 issues)
☐ Large Print *Every Day with Jesus* (1yr, 6 issues)
☐ *Inspiring Women Every Day* (1yr, 6 issues)
☐ *Life Every Day* (Jeff Lucas) (1yr, 6 issues)

☐ *Mettle*: 14-18s (1yr, 3 issues)
☐ *YP's*: 11-15s (1yr, 6 issues)
☐ *Topz*: 7-11s (1yr, 6 issues)

**Issue to commence fro**
☐ Jan/Feb ☐ Jul/Aug
☐ Mar/Apr ☐ Sep/Oct
☐ May/Jun ☐ Nov/Dec

**CWR**     Instruction to your Bank or Building Society to pay by Direct Debit     **DIRECT Debit**

Please fill in the form and send to: CWR, Waverley Abbey House, Waverley Lane, Farnham, Surrey GU9 8EP

Name and full postal address of your Bank or Building Society

To: The Manager     Bank/Building Society

Address _____

Postcode _____

Name(s) of Account Holder(s) _____

Branch Sort Code ☐☐ ☐☐ ☐☐

Bank/Building Society Account Number ☐☐☐☐☐☐☐☐

Originator's Identification Number **4 2 0 4 8 7**

Reference _____

Instruction to your Bank or Building Society
Please pay CWR Direct Debits from the account detailed in this Instruction subje to the safeguards assured by the Direct Debit Guarantee.
I understand that this Instruction may remain with CWR and, if so, details will be passed electronically to my Bank/Building Society.

Signature(s) _____

Date _____

Banks and Building Societies may not accept Direct Debit Instructions for some types of account

# New Resources

## Fleeting Shadows:
## How Christ transforms the darkness

In this *Cover to Cover* Lent study guide,
Malcolm Duncan draws from his own
life experience to help us reflect on the
cross and the power of Christ as we
walk through challenging trials and
tribulations.

Six weekly sessions, suitable for
individual and group use.

Author: Malcolm Duncan
ISBN: 978-1-78259-420-8

**£4.99 each**

## When Faith Gets Shaken DVD

Not final cover

Presented by: Patrick Regan
EAN: 5027957-001633

**£14.99 (inc VAT)**

This six-session DVD is presented by
Patrick Regan, CEO of XLP, and brings
alive, for small groups and individuals
alike, some honest reflections on
how we can focus on God and keep
going when our faith gets shaken.

Filmed on location in London, Patrick
uses Scripture, powerful personal
testimony as well as interviews with
friends, family members and colleagues
to lead us through how we can rethink
trust, peace, courage, surrender, guilt
and hope when we face uncertainties
and feel as though life is falling apart.

Includes on-screen discussion starters
to help you explore and hear what God
may be whispering along the way.

To order, visit **www.cwr.org.uk/store**, call **01252 784700** or
see the order form on the last page of this devotional.

The Bible is full of songs, and not all of them
are catchy. Some of them are triumphant
anthems of victory, sung when God delivered
people who were stranded and hopeless
without His intervention. Others are gut-
wrenchingly honest songs of lament, as
bruised and disappointed believers sang the
blues because God seemed distant. The songs
of the Bible give us keen insight into the reality
of the human condition, and shine light on the
beauty of God's character. Join Jeff as we tune
in to some of those biblical songs. Wherever
we are on our own faith journeys, the ancient
songs of Scripture can help us keep walking
forward with God today.

*Life Every Day* is written bimonthly by Jeff
Lucas to help you apply the Bible to your
everyday life. Through laughter, tears and
his customary wit and wisdom, Jeff will help
you day by day to gain insight, understanding
and practical application from God's Word.
Expect to be challenged, encouraged,
entertained and confronted.

International author, speaker
and broadcaster, Jeff Lucas
also holds a pastoral teaching
position at Timberline Church
in Colorado.

## Songs of Praise

**JAN/FEB 2016**

www.facebook.com/
jefflucasuk

**Website:** www.cwr.org.uk
**Email:** mail@cwr.org.uk

**UK EDITION: £2.99**

ISBN 978-1-78259-465-9

9 781782 594659

ALSO AVAILABLE AS
EMAIL SUBSCRIPTION/EBOOK/KINDLE

OTHER CWR DAILY BIBLE-READING NOTES

EVERY DAY
WITH JESUS

INSPIRING WOMEN
EVERY DAY

COVER TO COVER
EVERY DAY

Exodus 1-15
Mark 1-10

METTLE
14-18s

YP's
11-15s

TOPZ
7-11s

**Applying God's Word** *to everyday life and relationships*